Costume

Cally Blackman

Costume and clothes are the most visible means we have of expressing ourselves. For hundreds of years they have been used to signify status, power, political messages and wealth, while for ordinary people they have been adapted for various trades and professions. At the period when this guide begins, the 16th century, fashionable dress was the preserve of the privileged few. Only the wealthiest in the land – that is, royalty and the court – could afford to purchase the luxury fabrics, furs and jewels that cost many times more than the annual earnings of a working man. Conspicuous consumption was the most important ingredient in fashion.

Gradually, however, with the rise of the middle classes and general improvements in standards of living for most people over the centuries, it has become a commodity to which we can all aspire. In this way, the direction of the influence of fashion has been reversed – instead of fashionable trends being passed down from the higher echelons of society to the lower, the democratization of society and fashion means that innovation now often comes from street level.

Perhaps because very few people, past or present, are immune to the seduction of beautiful clothes, we can relate our own experience of fashionable dress to that of our ancestors – ephemeral though it might be, fashion is not only one of the most sensitive barometers of society, but it also touches all of our lives.

Front cover:
In this portrait, c.1755, by
Pickering, Eleanor Dixie
wears a sack dress
in a lightly sprigged floral
design. She draws on the
long gloves that were
an essential element of
formal dress.

Opposite:
The dense floral embroidery
on this jacket fabric, popular
in the early years of the
17th century, was unique
to England.

Right:
This enamelled cross, set
with rubies and a diamond,
was made in England in the
mid 16th century. It is on
display in the Victoria &
Albert Museum.

TUDOR MAGNIFICENCE AND ELIZABETHAN IMAGERY

1500—1600

*H*enry VIII's accession in 1509 introduced a renaissance in English cultural life, with the new king's court at its centre. Henry's love of splendour and luxury,

Henry VIII wears a sable-lined crimson gown with hanging sleeves embroidered in gold, and a full-skirted jerkin over a slashed and bejewelled gold brocade doublet. The prominent codpiece, massive bulk and dominant posture portray Henry's personification of Tudor power.

♦

his lavish entertainments and his patronage of education and the arts established the English court as the foremost in Western Europe, its only rival in magnificence being that of France. Henry loved display and used fine clothes, sumptuous fabrics, rich furs and magnificent jewels to reinforce his image, firstly of a youthful Renaissance prince and later as a mature and dominating king. A wealthy landowning class emerged as a result of the dissolution of the monasteries. However, life was still hard for

The construction of the ba of the English hood is clear seen in this drawing by Holbein. The lappets at th side are pinned up over th ears and are probably mad of gold brocaded fabric.

♦

many – unemployment, inflation and disease were rife.

Male dress, more extravagant than female during Henry's reign, consisted of five basic layered garments – gown, jerkin, doublet, hose and shirt. Sumptuous Italian fabrics were used for outer garments – the gown could be lined with fur and encrusted with embroidery, gold braid and jewels. The jerkin and doublet were slashed to reveal contrasting linings or shirt linen pulled through the slits. The hose consisted of an upper and lower part, joined together until the 1570s, attached to the inside of the doublet by ties tipped with metal points, or 'aglets'. The shirt was embroidered and frilled at collar and cuffs. Hats were worn inside and out; usually made of blocked felted wool, the upturned brim was pinned with jewels and trimmed with ostrich feathers. The look was one of masculine swagger and bulk.

Pendants were a favourite Renaissance jewel; in this example, designed by Holbein, an elaborately scrolled and enamelled background is set with gemstones and pearls.

◆

Catherine Parr, Henry VIII's last wife, wears a magnificent silver brocade gown. The sleeves are lined with lynx; the red velvet undersleeves and forepart are embroidered in gold thread and pearls with an intricate design of lovers' knots.

◆

Women wore a dress called a 'kirtle', under a full, trained gown. The kirtle had a rigid bodice with a low, square neckline and a gored skirt that could be left open at the front, forming an inverted triangle to display a contrasting petticoat, or 'forepart'. The wide oversleeves of the gown were turned back above the elbow to show off their contrasting lining. The bosom was covered with a piece of fine lawn edged with embroidery, a 'partlet', while the shift frill was allowed to show around the neckline. The gable, or English hood, fashionable until the 1530s, was a rigid structure framing the face with a black velvet cap enclosing the head, ending in two long bands sometimes worn pinned up. Under this, a linen coif covered the hair. Jewellery consisted of fine chain necklaces, pendants, brooches and beaded girdles. The neckline, or 'square', was often edged with jewels, as was the 'billiment', or outer edge, of the headdress.

Tudor Magnificence and Elizabethan Imagery

Spanish dress, distinctively formal, became a significant influence on mid-century fashion and was adopted in territories ruled by the Habsburg dynasty, to which Spain, hitherto an isolated country, now belonged. England was not immune to its influence; through Catherine of Aragon and her daughter Mary I, whose marriage to Philip II in 1554 briefly united the two countries, Spanish styles became the height of fashion at court. 'Spanish black' and a muted palette, expressions of sober luxury, replaced the jewel-like colours of Henry VIII's time (Spain held the monopoly on South American logwood, the best black dyestuff).

Caps like this were worn by men at home, not in bed but as informal wear for comfort and warmth. This one is embroidered with a design of flowers and scrolling stems.

✦

This young lady's embroidered bodice sleeve are matched by the partle Gold-edged ruff and cuff encircle her neck and wris Her velvet cap, worn ove a red coif, is pinned with jewels and a feather pompom.

✦

Men wore a Spanish cloak instead of an overgown, a sleeveless leather jerkin and a more fitted doublet with 'pickadils' at the waist. Women, who had by c.1545 adopted the Spanish farthingale, wore a separate bodice and skirt with a fitted overgown for extra warmth. Both sexes favoured the Spanish figure-of-eight style of ruff.

Despite high taxes, the Elizabethan period saw increased spending on clothes, indulged in by both the aristocratic and the burgeoning yeomen and merchant classes. Elizabeth's accession heralded a love of bright, fresh colours, and a passion for embroidery, an essential part of every woman's education; applied to every garment in the wardrobe, its motifs were loaded with symbolism and meaning which have to be decoded in order to fully understand dress at this time.

NON SINE SOLE
IRIS.

In this portrait, Elizabeth I grasps a rainbow, the symbol of peace after storms. The embroidered serpent on her sleeve signifies prudence and passion, while the ears and eyes on her mantle represent her omniscience and discernment. Pearls denote her virginity.

◆

This elegant young courtier poses with a melancholic air in his short doublet with its peascod belly, a cartwheel ruff and a short, fur-lined cloak nonchalantly slung over one shoulder.

◆

Dress Code

The arts of poetry, hidden meanings, coded messages and courtly love were highly developed and reflected in fashionable dress at Elizabeth's court – knotwork, flowers, animals, insects and natural phenomena, allegorical emblems, personal devices and colours carried specific meanings or references. All of these would have been familiar to contemporary observers, but to our untrained eyes much of their significance is lost.

The most important change in women's dress during Elizabeth's reign was the introduction of the French drum-shaped farthingale in the 1590s, worn under the skirt (petticoat), now separate from the bodice. The bodice, stiffened at the front by a triangular stomacher, extended in a long point over the petticoat. The width of the farthingale was balanced by the ever widening ruff and enormous sleeves, padded out in a tubular shape. Hair, dressed high on top of the head, was pinned with jewels and feathers. Lead-based make-up was worn to lighten the skin, and veins on the neck and bosom were painted in blue to heighten the effect.

Children's Dress

Babies were swaddled for a few weeks, then both sexes were put into 'frocks' with hanging sleeves that doubled up as leading reins. The equivalent of our modern-day nappy was simply a piece of linen, probably cut from outworn garments, called a 'tailclout'. Pieces of coral made into teething rings or rattles with bells were believed to ward off diseases and bring luck. From about the age of six or seven, boys were 'breeched' – that is, they were put into a scaled-down version of adult male dress. Little girls also wore adult styles from about the age of five, sometimes earlier, wearing boned stays and bodices according to fashion. Children did not wear specialized clothing until the end of the 18th century.

In this portrait of Charles I's three eldest children, the future Charles II and his sister Mary are wearing adult dress, but their brother James, being only two years old, has not yet been breeched and is still wearing a frock.

✦

The two young boys in this detail from a portrait of the Lucy family are wearing frocks with leading strings attached at the shoulders. The starched, ruff-like collars were soon to be replaced by the softer, more comfortable, falling collar.

✦

1600—1700

Embroidered jackets were worn at home informally, for comfort; coloured silks, silver lace and spangles ensured that they were still very decorative. Margaret Laton's jacket, shown here, survives in the Victoria & Albert Museum.

✦

Domestic peace and a rapid expansion in urban population growth during the first forty years of the 17th century saw merchants and tradesmen prosper, and the growth of the landed gentry class. Imported goods from the New World were available at shops in the larger towns; commerce was enhanced by improved methods of transport.

The tendency towards a poetic notion of melancholic effeminacy in male dress during Elizabeth I's reign reached a crescendo during the reign of James I. The foppish king, 'the wisest fool in Christendom', surrounded by his male favourites, encouraged an air of decadence at his court rarely seen before, or since. This was reflected in fashions which became ever more extravagant until the accession in 1625 of Charles I, who, with his queen, Henrietta Maria, introduced a taste for more sophisticated, plainer French styles at court. Until then, the Jacobean passion for surface decoration held sway – polychrome embroidery covered outer garments, while underclothes and coifs were decorated in the more restrained blackwork.

Gloves were presented as tokens of esteem, traditionally by or to the sovereign on New Year's Day. Made of buff leather with long, tapering fingers and embroidered gauntlets, they were often scented with sandalwood.

✦

The 3rd Earl of Dorset's wealth and importance are highlighted in this dazzling display of Jacobean dress. Every item is decorated, from the collar, edged with spiky Italian reticella lace, to the stockings with their embroidered clocks.

✦

Excess, Revolution and Restoration

A prudish family man, Charles and his queen did away with the sartorial excesses of his father's court. It is clear from his wardrobe accounts that Charles was interested in clothes, however, and the devoted couple set about leading the trend in romantic, 'cavalier' fashions. Exuberant surface decoration gave way to lustrous silks and satins in russet browns, sulphur yellows, rich blues and greens and muted greys and black. The sheen of fabric was more important than surface decoration, though it was enlivened by pinking, slashing, trimmings of braid, ribbon bows and rosettes. Lace, an extremely costly accessory, was worn in profusion, edging collars, caps, cuffs, handkerchiefs and boothose.

Queen Henrietta Maria wears a shimmering green satin gown with a high-waisted bodice, embroidered with pearls. The exquisite lace collar and cuffs and the coral-pink ribbon at her waist, matching the fan, lighten the effect.

◆

This gentlewoman wears her gown kilted up over a richly embroidered petticoat. Her shoes, trimmed with rosettes, and the deep-brimmed hat indicate that she is a wealthy merchant's wife.

◆

Men wore cloaks over their high-waisted doublets with tabs at the waist and longer, slimmer breeches. By the early 1630s the ruff was replaced by a wide, lace-edged falling collar, worn by both men and women. Lace-edged boothose were worn inside boots with wide cuffs at the top and butterfly straps to which spurs were attached. The romantic look was completed by a wide-brimmed hat decorated with a plume of ostrich feathers and natural shoulder-length curls, waxed moustaches and pointed beards.

Women could wear either a low-necked bodice, sometimes worn with a folded kerchief for modesty, or a doublet-style jacket, fastening high at the neck. Both had a tabbed basque at the bottom and were worn with gently rounded skirts, shaped over hip pads. The high, frizzed hairstyle popular in James I's reign gave way to small buns, curls and ringlets, while pearls, their sheen enhanced by the glossy silks and satins that were worn, made up the most fashionable jewellery. Women loved to wear masculine styles; as well as the doublet style of bodice, the wide-brimmed beaver hat could be worn with a swagger, attracting criticism from Puritan moralists, a reflection of the growing unpopularity of the court and its fashions.

In this portrait of Lord John Stuart and his brother, the high-waisted, slashed satin doublets, the cloaks and the breeches trimmed with ribbon and lace sum up the careless elegance of the cavalier court.

◆

Behind the Masque

The most popular form of entertainment was the masque, which involved the design of complicated moving sets and fanciful costumes based on the contemporary idea of classical dress. Many of these were designed by the architect Inigo Jones, and members of the court, including the king and queen, took part in these entertainments. However, political and civil unrest was soon to put an end to the extravagances of court life.

Queen Anne of Denmark, James I's consort, is depicted as a Winged Masquer in a masque designed by Inigo Jones.

◆

Excess, Revolution and Restoration

Charles II's coronation robes comprised an ermine-lined cloak and surcoat over silver tissue petticoat breeches, trimmed with loops of ribbon. The short sleeves of the doublet display the lace-trimmed cuffs. Across his chest is the Order of the Garter sash.

✦

The hiatus of the Civil War did not disrupt the onward march of fashion as much as might be imagined; people on both sides continued to consume fashion according to their status and wealth. The main impact of the war, and the ensuing Commonwealth and Protectorate periods, was an emphasis on more subdued colours, plainer styles and trimmings. Men wore elements of military dress – the metal gorget and breastplate, buff leather jerkin and military sash can be seen in many portraits. However, images of Puritan or Parliamentarian dress are very rare. Puritan clothing, typified by the wearing of sombre black and the short, pudding-basin 'Roundhead' haircut (both taken from Protestant Dutch styles), was only worn by a small minority.

The Restoration of the monarchy in 1660 brought back with it not only a new king, but also a renewed love of luxury in dress. Having spent much of his exile at the court of Louis XIV, it was inevitable that Charles II would introduce fashions influenced by those worn in France. Wide petticoat breeches, or 'Rhinegraves', festooned with loops of ribbon and bows, were worn with a doublet by now so short that acres of shirt were visible between the two. However, in 1666 an important development took place in male fashion when the king introduced a more rational form of dress at court – a long coat worn over an equally long, sleeved vest, or waistcoat, worn over slimmer breeches. The vest, fastened with a profusion of buttons, probably derived from Persian clothing. Natural 'cavalier' hairstyles were literally replaced by luxuriant, curled 'full-bottomed' wigs, which, until well into the next century, became essential features of male dress.

Sir Robert Vyner wears an informal silk dressing gown while Lady Vyner wears a stiff bodice and striped silk petticoat under her silk over gown. The children wear more formal versions of adult dress, though their daughter still retains the leading strings of childhood.

◆

A fashionable French mantua is shown in this engraving, with a frill, or 'falbala', decorating the petticoat, and a commode headdress. At the end of the 17th century, engravings depicting fashion became popular in France.

◆

The loosely draped gowns and revealing chemises depicted on the beauties of Charles' court did not reflect actual clothing style. Typical of the *déshabillé* we associate with the relaxed moral atmosphere during his reign, these were an attempt on the part of the portrait painter to convey his notion of romanticized classical dress. In reality, women wore an increasingly long, front-fastening, boned bodice over a trained skirt pinned up at the side to display an ornate petticoat underneath. This style was eventually replaced by a new type of gown, the mantua, which became a staple in the female wardrobe for many years. By the 1690s, the hair was being arranged in a 'tower' or 'commode' headdress, adorned with wired tiers of lace and ribbon.

These shoes, made of blue velvet and embroidered with silver-gilt thread, are thought to have been worn by Lady Mary Stanhope around 1660, the time of Charles II's restoration.

◆

1700—1800

The influence on fashion of casual country clothing is illustrated in this portrait by Gainsborough. Mr Andrews wears a double-breasted frock-coat, while his wife wears a jacket and skirt over wide, square hoops, and a cap under her straw hat.

✦

A short, powdered wig replaced the full-bottomed wig in the 1720s. Here, the 'queue' at the back of the head is visible.

✦

$\mathcal{D}$espite the instabilities bequeathed to the nation at the end of the 17th century – disputed inheritance to the throne, religious divisions, war with France and the continuing poverty of the working classes – for many, the 18th century was a period of cultural enrichment, improved education and political stability brought about by the successive reigns of the three Hanoverian Georges. One of the most elegant periods in our history, it was a time when the impetus of fashion, dominated by French influence, became unstoppable. Increased prosperity, improved communications, foreign travel and avid consumption of luxury goods meant that styles changed more rapidly than before.

The male suit varied in minor details only – the cut of a sleeve, the length of waistcoat, the choice of fabric were the only variables, though generally it became less bulky and slimmer in fit with the front edges of the coat curving towards the back. As the century progressed, there was an increasing preference for informal clothing derived from elements of country clothing and working dress – Lord Chesterfield complained in the 1740s that young men-about-town were wearing the dress of 'grooms, stagecoachmen

This magnificent brocaded silk dress with square side hoops would have been worn for a special court occasion, such as one of the royal birthdays.

✦

Caps were essential wear for women, both indoors and out. Here, a lace cap is worn with the lappets hanging down at the back.

✦

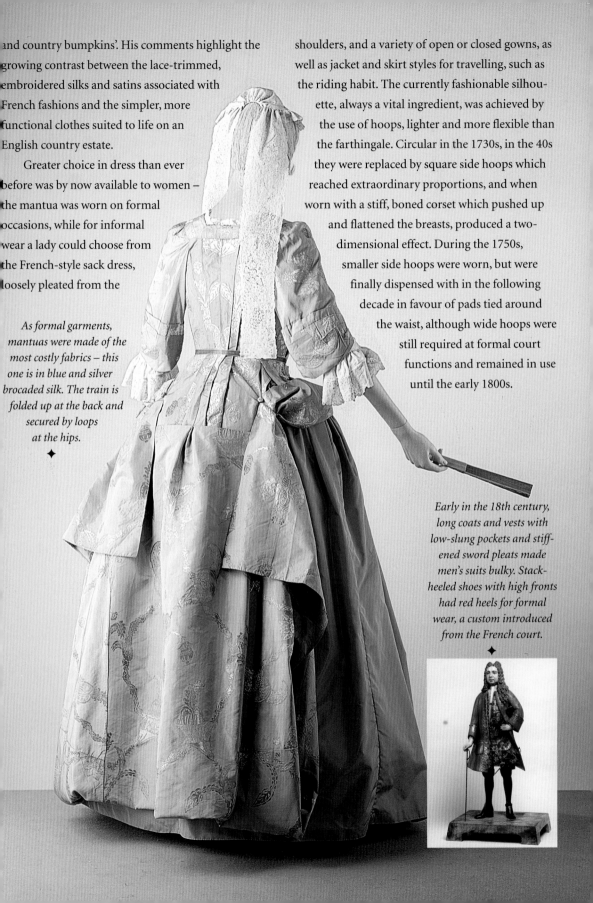

and country bumpkins'. His comments highlight the growing contrast between the lace-trimmed, embroidered silks and satins associated with French fashions and the simpler, more functional clothes suited to life on an English country estate.

Greater choice in dress than ever before was by now available to women – the mantua was worn on formal occasions, while for informal wear a lady could choose from the French-style sack dress, loosely pleated from the

shoulders, and a variety of open or closed gowns, as well as jacket and skirt styles for travelling, such as the riding habit. The currently fashionable silhouette, always a vital ingredient, was achieved by the use of hoops, lighter and more flexible than the farthingale. Circular in the 1730s, in the 40s they were replaced by square side hoops which reached extraordinary proportions, and when worn with a stiff, boned corset which pushed up and flattened the breasts, produced a two-dimensional effect. During the 1750s, smaller side hoops were worn, but were finally dispensed with in the following decade in favour of pads tied around the waist, although wide hoops were still required at formal court functions and remained in use until the early 1800s.

As formal garments, mantuas were made of the most costly fabrics – this one is in blue and silver brocaded silk. The train is folded up at the back and secured by loops at the hips.

◆

Early in the 18th century, long coats and vests with low-slung pockets and stiffened sword pleats made men's suits bulky. Stack-heeled shoes with high fronts had red heels for formal wear, a custom introduced from the French court.

◆

Suzanna Beckford wears a formal open sack of watered silk decorated with serpentine-ruched robings on the stomacher and at the sides of the front. The sleeve ruffles, necklace and kerchief are in matching lace fabric.

✦

The Age of Elegance

During the middle of the 18th century the rococo style, as popularized by Madame de Pompadour, the French King Louis XV's mistress, swept through all the decorative arts. Curving lines, asymmetrical details, floral motifs and a new lightness of decoration were all typical of the Romantic naturalism associated with the period. This elegance was expressed in female dress through the use of floral patterned silks, frills and flounces, masses of ribbon and lace trimmings, costly accessories such as fans, and high hairstyles pinned with flowers and feathers. For outdoors, a flattish straw hat tied with ribbon was worn, tilting forwards on the head to accommodate the hair. Much jewellery was worn, especially at court, such as a parure – a matching set of earrings, necklace and bracelets. Stomachers were covered in brilliant-cut diamonds and brooches scattered across the surface of a gown. Paste – clear glass stones mounted over coloured foils – was highly valued in its own right and imitated the sparkle of diamonds as it reflected the light of hundreds of candles at social gatherings.

Scientific discovery, invention and entrepreneurism began to fuel the 'long Industrial Revolution'. Industrialists such as Josiah Wedgwood, Matthew Boulton and Sir Richard Arkwright encouraged the influx of a previously rural workforce into the towns. An increase in disposable income fostered new kinds of public entertainment – masquerades and subscription balls were held, while pleasure gardens, such as those at Ranelagh and Vauxhall in London, and watering places, or

Young men who went to Europe on the Grand Tour to improve their education brought back Continental influences – the most extreme of these, the 'macaronis', wore brightly coloured, tight, effeminate styles, much lampooned in the popular press.

✦

In the mid 1770s, exaggerated hairstyles were fashionable – the hair, powdered and glued with pomatum made from gum arabic, was adorned with ribbons, feathers and flowers. Coloured powder was sometimes used.

✦

Sumptuous Silks

The most desirable brocaded silks were made in Lyons and were often brought back as gifts by visitors to the Continent. However, at the end of the 17th century the influx from France of Huguenot refugees, gifted at silk-weaving and silversmithing, ensured a competitive domestic trade. Spitalfields silks were renowned for their delicate tracery of flowers, scrolls and stripes.

spas, afforded the opportunity to promenade in the latest fashions. For the first time, British male fashion began to influence the rest of Europe – even France, where up to and after the Revolution the extravagant clothing worn by aristocrats began to be perceived as positively undesirable. The firmly entrenched British tradition of governmental democracy based on the land-owning classes was reflected by its style of dress. Dark, well-cut suits in English woollen fabrics, or frock-coats worn with revealing buff breeches and riding boots, caped greatcoats and round-brimmed hats worn without powdered wigs became *à la mode* across the Continent by the end of the century.

This portrait of Mr and Mrs Coltman, by Joseph Wright of Derby, depicts 18th-century casual dress. Women wore the riding habit not only for riding, but also for walking, visiting and at home before changing for dinner.

◆

These blue silk shoes, decorated with silver metal thread and spangles, would have fastened over the tongue with a buckle.

◆

The Age of Elegance

By the 1780s rococo had been superseded by neo-classicism, a result of the excavation of Greek and Roman sites such as Pompeii and Herculaneum. Classical simplicity in dress was now the desired effect, and brocaded silk was abandoned in favour of diaphanous muslins, sprigged cottons and spotted dimities imported from India. The 'chemise' dress was the most significant development in female fashion at this period. Made in sheer white muslin, with its waistline high under the bust, it recalled in its simplicity the costume worn in Greek statuary and vases. At first, it was thought to be shocking because of its close resemblance to an undergarment, but it soon became the most fashionable type of dress until the early years of the next century. The high hairstyles of the 1770s and 80s, towering edifices dressed with pomade and powder and festooned with trimmings sometimes relating to topical events, were replaced by a more natural curled or frizzed look, though powder was still widely used.

The trend-setting Duchess of Devonshire was the first lady in Britain to wear the chemise dress, seen here in a portrait drawn by John Downman in 1787.

◆

Stockings gartered above the knee are visible in this detail of Hogarth's painting from The Rake's Progress. *The prostitute's stays lie on the floor at her side.*

◆

A linen shift is worn under the red silk damask corset which is stiffened with strips of whalebone, while the cane side hoops are covered in pink-striped linen.

◆

Linen was always worn next to the skin to protect the over garments from soiling. Over her long chemise, often beautifully embroidered or edged with lace, a woman would wear stays, made of stout linen cloth, reinforced by whalebone strips. These were traditionally made by men because of the strength required to shape and sew them. Sometimes they were made of leather, particularly for working women.

During the first half of the 16th century, the Spanish farthingale was worn under the petticoat, giving a bell-like silhouette. This was replaced in the 1590s by the French wheel, or drum, farthingale. Pads or cork 'bum rolls' were worn during the 17th century, giving a more gently rounded effect, but early in the 18th century, square hoops were adopted. Although these diminished in size in fashionable dress as the century progressed, they were retained for court wear for many years.

Men wore a long shirt under the doublet, tucked into the trunkhose and later the breeches. Extra warmth was sometimes provided by wearing a knitted jacket under the doublet as well.

For both men and women, silk or wool knitted stockings were rolled over the knee and kept in place by a garter. These were often beautifully embroidered with clocks at the side of the leg. During the 17th century, men could also wear lace-trimmed boothose which were turned over the top of the boots.

The male version of déshabillé, *the night-gown, or dressing gown, worn at home for comfort and warmth, must have been a relief from more formal dress. They were often made in exotic silks imported from the Far East.*

◆

DOMESTICITY AND THE INDUSTRY OF FASHION

A huge variety of goods, from British manufacturing centres and from all over the world, became available in shops – one shop even claimed that it could supply 'every article of foreign manufacture which there is any possibility of obtaining'.

✦

1800—1900

This 1844 family portrait shows a variety of dress. The older woman still wears the fashions of her youth, while the younger women are more up-to-date – deep lace 'bertha' collars over bodices with a long, pointed front.

✦

Appliqué floral motifs decorate the hem of this evening dress of 1815, showing the move away from classical simplicity to the more romantic fashions of the second decade of the century.

✦

𝐵y the beginning of the 19th century, the Industrial Revolution was gathering pace, the mechanization of the textile industry being one of its main driving forces. Manchester's cotton and linen mills, Nottingham's lace factories, ribbon and silk manufacturing at Macclesfield and the woollen mills of Norwich and Paisley played their part in the industrialization of a formerly rural economy. The mass production of good-quality cotton and linen fabrics, which by 1783 could be printed by metal rollers, saw the demise in importation of Indian goods. It also meant that these fabrics were affordable for the working and middle classes; the fact that they could be washed, unlike silk, was an added bonus which resulted in an improvement in general standards of hygiene.

Shopping became a form of national entertainment – by the beginning of the century, gas lighting was widely used in the London shops, considered to be among the finest in Europe. Oxford Street, St James's, Pall Mall and Regent Street, completed in 1830, provided unparalleled opportunities for purchasing clothing and accessories.

For the first decade of the century, the white chemise-style dress remained the most fashionable for women. The little warmth they provided could be improved by the addition of a shawl (imported at first from India, then later made in Paisley and Norwich), a short spencer' or a 'pelisse'. Gradually the silhouette widened at top and bottom, giving an hourglass figure, the focus of attention being at the shoulders and exposed bosom. Surface decoration once more became evident, with appliqué motifs applied at the shorter hemline, from which dainty feet in satin pumps appeared. Indoors, the hair could be dressed in an 'Apollo knot' on top of the head or, less formally, a frilled cap was worn, while for outdoors a face-framing bonnet tied with ribbon under the chin was essential. Jewellery drew inspiration from classical or historical sources.

As male tailoring reached new heights of sophistication by the turn of the century, the dandy came into being. Beau Brummell, friend of the Prince Regent, epitomized the English style - perfect fit, attention to detail, spotless white linen and a faultlessly tied cravat were among the high standards demanded by this arbiter of fashion. Breeches were replaced, at first by pantaloons then, by 1825, with trousers, which were originally worn only by working men and boys.

Left: The hourglass shape of fashionable female dress was echoed by men's – here, coats with tightly clinched waists and puffed sleeves, worn with silk top hats, epitomize the dandified look of the early 19th century.

◆

These dresses from the last quarter of the century show the wealth of detail and decoration fashionable during this period. Frills, flounces, braid, ribbon, fringing and lace proliferate.

◆

The complex drapery and trimming of 1870s fashion are shown in this painting. Pastel silks are offset by black velvet ribbons tied around the neck and wrists. The hair is dressed in a high chignon.

◆

Domesticity and the Industry of Fashion

Throughout the 19th century, rapidly changing styles in dress were disseminated by an ever-increasing number of newspapers, magazines, journals and pocketbooks aimed at followers of fashion. General improvements in transport, particularly the coming of the railways, contributed not only to the countrywide movement of goods, but also to increased opportunity for travel for all.

Advances in textile technology and mechanization continued to contribute to mass production of clothing, while in the domestic sphere the invention of the sewing machine by Elias Howe in 1845 in the USA, soon after marketed in Britain by Singer, saved hours of laborious hand sewing, enabling women to keep up with the latest fashions economically at home. The divergence of the role of the sexes in Victorian society was reflected in dress – male clothing, increasingly standardized and sober, expressed the new concept of the professional man. Women, as mere dependents, were expected to be decorative accessories, hidebound by the numerous changes of dress required in the course of the day according to strict codes of convention, which in turn ensured a high consumption of fashion.

The invention in 1856 of the crinoline, a light, sprung-wire cage, freed women from layers of cumbersome petticoats – up to as many as five – worn to achieve the required fullness of the skirt. The circular shape produced by the crinoline was modified in the 1860s to give more emphasis at the back of the skirt, and by the 1870s a bustle was worn alone under a flat-fronted skirt with complex drapery, trimmed with pleats and

Bicycling was one of the outdoor leisure pursuits that were eagerly taken up by women. Male dress was followed as far as possible – some daring women even wore knickerbockers – the only concessions to femininity were the leg-of-mutton sleeved jacket and the skirt.

◆

flounces, below a long fitted bodice with a square neckline. Despite the benefits of the sewing machine, the garment trade was rife with sweated labour; dressmakers, seamstresses and tailors worked long hours in bad conditions to meet the voracious demands of the customer. The fashion for surface decoration in the form of embroidery, beading, fringing, tassels and lace still required hours of manual work.

During his lecture tour of America in 1882, Oscar Wilde wore aesthetic dress to promote his 'unconventional' image – black breeches, a lounge jacket with quilted collar and cuffs, silk stockings and patent evening pumps decorated with bows.

✦

A Life of Leisure

During the last twenty years of the century, there was a general simplification in dress, partly in response to the efforts of dress reformers (who believed contemporary dress was ugly or injurious to health), and partly as a result of changing lifestyles. By the 1890s, increasing numbers of people were taking part in pastimes such as bicycling; the more relaxed garments worn for sport and leisure pursuits were to have a tremendous influence on fashion in the following century.

This 'tailormade' is typical of women's clothing at the turn of the century. Masculine elements are combined with practicality and physical freedom, encouraged by sport, dress reform and the struggle for female emancipation.

✦

In Mourning

Queen Victoria, in deepest mourning two years after Prince Albert's death, wears a dress and jacket made from crape fabric, and a white Marie Stuart mourning cap with a widow's peak covered with a black veil.

✦

It was during the 19th century that the cult of mourning reached its peak, largely owing to the influence of Queen Victoria, who, from the death of her husband Prince Albert in 1861 until her own death in 1901, plunged herself into black. A strict set of rules was applied to dress that should be worn during the various stages. For example, in 1876 a widow had to wear deep mourning for a year and a day, then second mourning for nine months, followed by ordinary mourning for three months and half mourning for six months, during which time she could wear grey, white or mauve. Jewellery was not allowed until the second stage – jet was very popular, as were memorial pieces containing a lock of the loved-one's hair. Mourning crape, a dull, crinkly fabric, mass-manufactured by Courtaulds, was the most widely used fabric to make mourning clothes, and department stores such as Peter Robinson specialized in supplying them at very short notice. Hearses, drawn by horses with black plumes and blackened harness, were followed by male mourners who wore black top hats with crape bands tied around them. Enormous amounts of money were spent on funerals, and many people who could barely afford it paid into cooperative societies to ensure a good send-off.

FLAPPERS, MODERN WOMEN AND RADICAL FASHION

1900—2000

The awkward stance produced by the S-bend corset can be seen in this illustration of shopping at Harrods, c.1910. Picture hats trimmed with ribbons and feathers accommodate the top-heavy hairstyles of the period.

✦

The fashionable Prince of Wales, later Duke of Windsor, was a trend-setter throughout his life. Here, he wears a Fair Isle sweater with plus fours, a soft-collared shirt, knitted stockings and a flat tweed cap.

✦

For the upper classes, the Edwardian era (1901–10) was unparalleled in opulence. The king, Edward VII, unlike his more sedate mother, enjoyed an unceasing round of social activity – house parties, shooting weekends, court functions, balls and dinners. Society women could purchase fashionable clothing from a couturier, an unknown phenomenon until the middle of the previous century. Paris became the hub of the fashion empire; its couture houses began to produce seasonal collections attracting a wealthy clientele from the USA and Europe.

Female enfranchisement and emancipation, fought for by the suffragettes, brought new freedoms. Single women, liberated from the domestic environment, began to go out to work or attend university or art school. Despite this, pre-war fashions were constricting – the S-bend corset and wasp waist produced one of the most awkward shapes that fashion has ever decreed, while the hobble skirt, introduced in 1910, further restricted movement. The Russian Ballet inspired a vogue for all things Oriental – vibrant new colours, harem trousers worn under tunics, turbans and black kohl-rimmed eyes, influencing the vampish heroines of the silent movies. With the outbreak of the First World War, the spirit of fashion was dampened. Women who joined in the war effort required more practical clothing, with some, such as those working in munitions factories or on the land, wearing trousers.

Camille Clifford, a comedy actress, epitomizes the curvaceous lines of the Edwardian era. The dress extends out in a swathe of fabric at the hem, while the hat and fan reflect the popularity of ostrich feathers as trimmings.

✦

Flappers, Modern Women and Radical Fashion

During 'The Roaring Twenties', a boyish look was the rage – hair was bobbed, 'flatteners' were worn to conceal the figure, and hemlines went above the knee in 1927. Tunic tops, blouses and jumpers, sometimes knitted, were worn long over the hips; hats consisted of head-hugging cloches. However, by the end of the decade a more sophisticated, modern look emerged. Femininity was once more desirable – sleek, streamlined dresses cut on the bias in floaty, printed fabrics with flared hemlines, or sophisticated tailored suits worn with witty little hats.

For upper-class men, fashion remained static, the formal suit being the linchpin of their wardrobe; but alongside the dark business suit, more relaxed, informal clothing could be worn,

This advertisement for Harvey Nichols shows an elegant fur-collared wrap coat, fashionable during the 1950s.

✦

Lounging pyjamas became fashionable during the 1920s for informal wear. These, in blue satin embroidered with dragons, were probably imported from the Far East.

✦

In this illustration, 'Ladies and Gentlemen in Evening Dress', several of the women's dresses have 'handkerchief' – uneven – hems, reflecting the varying dress lengths of the period. The gentlemen wear sharply cut evening suits with white waistcoats.

✦

uch as lounge suits in tweeds, or blazers and flannels, ith an increasing number of hat styles. American shion was particularly influential in casual wear, hile the outfits worn by glamorous Hollywood stars ere eagerly followed in the movies and magazines.

At the outbreak of the Second World War, restric- ons were placed on the purchase of textiles and othing; but, as ever, fashion did not stop at the onset f war. Great ingenuity was applied to maintaining a ylish appearance, while the influence of military

Left: The shorter, boxier coats and dresses that were fashionable during the Second World War were dictated by clothes rationing. The Board of Trade booklet 'Make Do and Mend' advised women on how to mend and renovate garments.

◆

Above: The inter-war years saw a general relaxation in menswear. Fluid fabrics and a more generous cut made clothing more comfortable. Broad shoulders, narrow waists and deep lapels reflect the influence of sophisticated modern American tailoring.

◆

Cutting the Cloth

Clothes rationing, established from 1941 to 1949, allowed at first for the consumption of about half the amount of clothing normally bought in peacetime and subsequently was reduced further. The supply of cloth was limited – as a result, hemlines became shorter and jack- ets boxier, while men's suits became two-piece and trousers were no longer permitted to have turn-ups. The utility scheme ensured that good standards were applied to consumer goods, including clothes.

wear showed itself in the use of belts, square-cut shoulders and breast pockets.

Dior's New Look collection, launched in 1947, caused a sensation with its lavish use of fabric, shock- ing for many who had scrimped and saved through- out the war years. His elegant, feminine silhouette, with cinched-in waist and rounded shoulders and hips, set a new style for the post-war years. Severely elegant, pencil-slim daywear styles ran in tandem with full-skirted dresses and lavish evening wear. The 1950s were the heyday of couture houses catering to a wealthy international clientele, though the influence of more casual, relaxed ready-to-wear American clothing was very significant.

Flappers, Modern Women and Radical Fashion

The Establishment of fashion was about to be challenged, however. Beatniks and art students emerging from regenerated post-war educational institutions were in the vanguard of the 'youthquake' that was to take place in the 1960s with 'Swinging London' at its epicentre. Young British designers in particular, such as Mary Quant, credited with the innovative miniskirt around 1965, brought in fashions aimed specifically at young people, who up until this time had had little choice but to dress similarly to their parents. In response, some Parisian couture houses launched cheaper, ready-to-wear lines, but London became the trend-setting capital of the world.

The youth movement, involved in political and student unrest, often expressed through the new medium of pop music, brought together the twin cultures of music and fashion. In the hippy capital of San Francisco, flower-power bloomed and pop groups that dabbled in Eastern mysticism popularized ethnic clothing. In Britain, designers such as Bill Gibb and Zandra Rhodes made colourful, mix-and-match patterned clothes trimmed with beads and feathers, while high-street fashion was led by boutiques such as Biba, whose twenties-inspired look – vampish eye make-up, cloche hats and all – was typical of the Swinging Sixties. Suddenly, strict codes of dress, still in force in the previous decade, were under threat and, for the first time, what was worn on the streets began to influence designers rather than vice versa.

The Biba look was influenced by nostalgia for the 1920s. Here, a crêpe tunic blouse is worn over wide, floppy trousers accessorized by a white silk fringed man's evening scarf. Huge khol-rimmed eyes complete the effect.

♦

Mary Quant was the most influential young designer in the 1960s. Her boutique, Bazaar, on the Kings Road, was a mecca for the 'in crowd', who wanted something more exciting than the matronly styles worn by their mothers.

♦

Well-established subcultural styles such as those worn by Teddy boys, mods and rockers were joined in the 1970s by a new wave of subversion in fashion. Punks paraded down the Kings Road, Chelsea, where the designer Vivienne Westwood had her boutique. Their anarchistic attitude set out to shock, but elements of their style were taken up by leading designers. Mainstream fashion in the 1980s reflected a more materialistic and image-conscious approach – power-dressing, typified by shoulder-padded suits, declared women's status as equal players in the world of business and politics. Sportswear became big business and infiltrated into high-street fashion.

By the end of the century, the concept of 'fashion' had fragmented and become, as never before, a matter of unlimited personal choice – today, individual identity can be expressed by choosing from a myriad of available styles. Yet the perennial demand for novelty in dress often relies on nostalgia; in this way, the history of fashion repeats itself and is always present.

The queen of punk fashion, Vivienne Westwood, has emerged as one of the most innovative British designers. Here, a tartan ensemble worn with black patent boots acknowledges British cultural heritage.

The Princess of Wales's patronage of British fashion designers gave the industry a boost. She caused a sensation when she wore this revealing off-the-shoulder dress by Christina Stambolian to a function at the Serpentine Gallery in London in 1992.

♦

Underwear up to 2000

*D*uring the 19th century, stays – now called corsets – continued to mould the female figure to whatever shape fashion decreed, while the pads that had until now been worn at the waist gave way to layers of heavy petticoats which were hot and uncomfortable, and soaked up rainwater from the ground. The light, sprung-wire crinoline, introduced in 1856, must have been a welcome relief. It was only in the early part of the 19th century that women started to wear 'drawers'; consequently the shift became shorter and evolved into the various types of undergarments, such as camisoles, that we associate with Victorian underwear.

The sharp contours of 195 fashion required strict underpinning. By now, th corset had separated int two parts – the brassiere a a roll-on girdle.

◆

This crinolinette shows the 90-degree angle produced by the bustle at the waist. The style was typical of the late 1880s.

◆

During the 1920s, underwear became much more flexible and comfortable as a result of advances in textile technology, including the development of elastic and synthetic fabrics such as rayon. The corset was eventually replaced by separate garments – the brassiere and the roll-on corset, to which suspenders were attached to support the stockings. The advent of the miniskirt increased the popularity of tights, first manufactured in 1960.

For men, the long shirt previously worn for hundreds of years diminished in size. Long underpants and long-sleeved vests were worn from the 19th century onwards, often made of wool because it was thought to be good for the health when worn next to the skin. During the 20th century these undergarments gradually became shorter and lighter, with cotton becoming the most popular fabric.

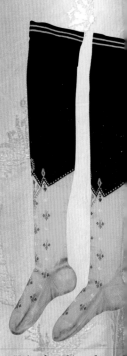

Knitted stockings from a periods were often elaborately decorated with wov or embroidered designs.

◆